OLLIE AND HARRY'S
MARVELOUS ADVENTURES

OLLIE AND HARRY'S MARVELOUS ADVENTURES

OLLIE FERGUSON & HARRY FERGUSON WITH MacNEILL FERGUSON

Norton Young Readers

An Imprint of W. W. Norton & Company
Independent Publishers Since 1923

Ollie & Harry: To Mummy and Daddy
MacNeill: To Vicki

Many of the experiments described in this book are suitable for children with adult supervision only. Please exercise common sense and use appropriate tools and well-fitting protective gear as/where needed. References to specific products, services, service providers and/or organizations are for illustration only and none should be read to suggest an endorsement or a guarantee of performance. Neither the publisher nor the author can guarantee the accuracy and completeness of this book for all purposes or make any representation with respect to the outcome of any project or instruction described. Web addresses appearing in this book reflect existing links as of the date of first publication. No endorsement of, or affiliation with, any third-party website should be inferred. Author and publisher are not responsible for third-party content (website, blog, information page, or otherwise). This book is sold without warranty of any kind, and none may be created or extended by sales representatives or written sales or promotional materials. Readers are solely responsible for ensuring that their activities comply with applicable law.

Contents

Introduction

Hello! We're Ollie and Harry. We live in Scotland, home of the Loch Ness Monster, the bagpipes, and the inventors of television, among many other cool things.

A few years ago we decided to create a list of adventures that we wanted to do before we turned eighteen years old. Our list started off short, but it quickly grew, and now we have five hundred adventures on it. Our Mum and Dad encouraged us to write the list, but they were a bit surprised when they saw it. They expected it to include "normal" things like canoeing, building a campfire, and perhaps even a bit of mountaineering. How wrong were they? Our list included launching Lego® figures into space and building a wildlife reserve.

Five years later, we're more than halfway through our list and have finished 270 adventures. On weekends and no-homework school nights, we've constructed a giant catapult, photographed the bottom of the ocean, and built an igloo. We've mummified a fish, hunted for meteorites, and even fired our Lego figures twenty miles (32 kilometers) into space. We got a photo of them hovering above Earth, and it was out of this world.

Our adventures have made us quite famous, and we've even been named Britain's Most Adventurous Boys. Our Facebook page, called "The Days Are Just Packed," has thousands of followers. Our best-known adventure—in which our toy pirate ship sailed all the way from Scotland to the Caribbean—was reported on TV and in newspapers in countries around the world, like France, Mexico, China, and the USA.

Our list has taught us about history, biology, geography, and zoology. We've learned to help others, overcome our fears, and be more aware of our environment. We've mastered some pretty cool

skills, too. How many other kids our age can start a fire with flint and steel, or can call an owl? Most important, we've had fun. A *lot* of fun.

This book is a guide to help you re-create some of our wildest and most fascinating adventures so far. You might think they'd be difficult, but take it from us—they aren't. All you need is a little organization and imagination, and you'll never have a dull weekend again.

A Note to Parents

In 2014, when my wife, Vicki, and I asked Ollie and Harry (then aged two and five) to come up with ideas for adventures they might like to do one weekend, we had no idea where it would lead us. The boys talked excitedly of expeditions into space and exploring the bottom of the ocean, celebrating intergalactic sausage day (an outdoor cookout involving "lorne" sausages, a local delicacy), and building an igloo to sleep in the snow. As the ideas kept coming, the list quickly grew to hundreds of adventures. It now stands at five hundred. As a family, we agreed to challenge ourselves to complete them by the time the boys turned eighteen. If nothing else, we reasoned, the four of us would spend time together, hopefully making incredible memories along the way.

Inevitably, the earliest adventures were appropriate for the boys' age, but as they've grown older their ideas have become grander in scope. We are great believers in giving Ollie and Harry the opportunity to experience the world around them without a thick padding of cotton wool, but this doesn't mean that we throw caution to the wind. On the contrary, we carefully weigh and manage the risk in each of their adventures, but you'd be surprised what children are capable of if you give them a little responsibility and allow them to develop common sense.

Our policy seems to have paid off, and we've all been rewarded. Some 270 adventures in, we are extraordinarily proud of the kind, resilient, and happy young boys they have become. Adventures have become an integral part of their childhood.

The adventures described in this book are guides only. You can adapt and modify them to your environment as needed—and in many cases, you will have to. You can also adapt them to your own parenting principles and draw your own lines in terms of risk.

To children, an adventure does not require scaling the highest mountain or reaching the North Pole. Children can find excitement in the smallest places—a creek in the woods or camping in a makeshift tent. However you approach them, I think you'll find that your children will derive joy and excitement from these adventures, and will make some magical memories, too.

—MacNeill Ferguson, Aberdeenshire, 2019

Ollie and Harry's (Boring but Very Important) Safety Notes

Before You Start

Like our dad said in his note to parents, your parents or whoever is responsible for you can trust you more than they might think. Still, there are some really important basic rules that you need to stick to when you're on any adventure, even if they sound stupid or totally obvious.

- Unless a parent or other adult is right there with you or you are a lot older than we are (seven and ten), and we do mean, a *lot* older, here are some things you really, really have to be sure you *don't* do.
    - make a fire, anywhere
    - use a knife or a power drill or a saw
    - melt metal, boil water, or cook anything
    - drive a tractor, even a small one
    - cut down or cut into a tree (or a fish, or anything else!)
- If you're really little, you may have to wait a while before you can do some of the things in this book, even with an adult around.
- Ask your parents or whoever is responsible for you if it's okay before you give out your email address to strangers and before you sign up on any website.
- If you are going anywhere alone, even for a few minutes, be sure to tell someone where you're going, bring your cell phone, and make sure it's charged. Even better, bring a charging cable and a power supply.
- If you're doing anything with goggles and gloves, make sure they fit you and make sure the gloves don't have holes.
- Don't go out in a boat unless you can swim, or you wear a life jacket.
- Don't try to get sap from a tree unless you have permission from whoever owns the property where the tree is.

The products we mention are ones that we liked and that worked for us. But you should always do your own research to find what will work for you.

EPIC SPACE ADVENTURE

Few of our adventures have been as exciting and spectacular as sending a balloon piloted by two Lego® figures into space—or the part of Earth's atmosphere called *near space*, to be precise. It took a lot of planning to get our homemade spacecraft and camera more than twenty miles (32 km) into the sky and then back to Earth again. Not only did we have to get hold of GPS equipment, a high-altitude balloon capable of making the trip, and a GoPro camera so that we could track and film its journey, we also had to plan the timing and judge the weather so that our spacecraft would land somewhere safe and on dry land. Last but not least, we had to get permission from the aviation authorities. This all took a couple of months to plan, but it was worth every ounce of effort. It was an extraordinary experience watching the big balloon climb high above us, slowly shrinking to the size of a small dot in the sky.

Recovering our spacecraft was an adventure in itself. After three and a half hours, we got a "ping" from the GPS tracking device that indicated our craft was falling to Earth and would land in a nearby town. We raced there, terrified that it would crash on a busy street, but there was no sign of it. It was only when we checked again that we realized we had tried to fix its landing spot too soon: it had still been a mile in the sky when we got the notification. It was now predicted to land five miles (eight kilometers) away, near a small village. It was almost dark by the time we found it, but Mum spotted something orange flapping in the wind in the middle of a plowed field. It was the parachute! We scrambled through the furrows to our rather muddy spaceship. To our amazement, nothing was broken, and the camera was still filming.

You can create a homemade spacecraft for your own out-of-this-world adventure. It requires careful planning and some special equipment, but watching a video of your astronauts hovering above Earth on the edge of space is an unforgettable experience!

What You'll Need

[ ] Styrofoam box

[ ] GoPro or other action camera

[ ] Satellite tracker or GPS locator

[ ] Astronaut or mascot

[ ] High-altitude parachute

[ ] Paracord (parachute cord)

[ ] High-altitude balloon

[ ] Helium gas and tubing

[ ] Hook scale or fishing scale

What to Do

1 **Check your local flying regulations and get permission to launch your spacecraft.** Wherever you are, the skies will probably be busy with other air traffic, so for the sake of safety, it's important to make sure that your craft isn't breaking any laws or posing a danger to others. You will first need to get permission from the authority controlling the air space where you plan to launch. In our case it was the CAA (Civil Aviation Authority), but in the US it is the FAA (Federal Aviation Administration). It isn't as hard as it sounds, though, as you just need to file the appropriate paperwork. Then, on the day of your flight, you may need to speak to your local airfield or airport to make sure you don't interfere with any aircraft in the area. As you can see, this adventure requires some patience, but this gives you plenty of time to perfect your space vehicle.

ABOUT HIGH-ALTITUDE BALLOONS

High-altitude balloons (also called weather or sounding balloons) come in various sizes and can be purchased online, together with accessories such as parachutes, paracord, and GPS devices. Many online high-altitude ballooning sites also offer tutorials and other useful information. Larger balloons can carry heavier loads and will rise higher before bursting, but they are also harder to handle and require more gas to inflate. For this flight, we used a 600-gram balloon. Helium can be rented from party supply and tool rental stores. Check to make sure that it is pure helium, as some party rental stores mix helium with nitrogen, which will cause the balloon to burst at a lower altitude.

2 **Make your spaceship.** Your "spaceship" will carry battery packs and locators and will protect your camera when it falls back to Earth. Styrofoam packing boxes are ideal as they are lightweight, strong, and waterproof. They are also cheap to buy and easy to cut holes in. Attach your camera to the inside of the box, then make a small hole through which it can record the journey. Ensure that the camera is positioned in a way that allows the best possible view of what's going on around it while minimizing its exposure to the freezing temperatures outside.

In the upper atmosphere, temperatures can drop to −4°F (−20°C), and the cold temperature and long flight time means you may need to use an extended-life battery in your camera. We used a GoPro camera with a waterproof housing to add some extra strength and protection. Secure your GPS or satellite locator inside the box and test all of the equipment to ensure that it works. Attach your "astronauts" to the outside of the craft. We put our two Lego men on an armature that protruded from the craft, and made sure they were in sight of the camera so that they provided a foreground to all the exciting action that would be going on in the background.

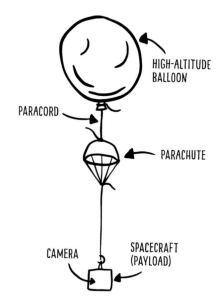

HIGH-ALTITUDE BALLOON

PARACORD

PARACHUTE

CAMERA

SPACECRAFT (PAYLOAD)

3 **Assemble.** Suspend your spacecraft below the parachute with approximately 10 feet (3 meters) of paracord, then suspend the parachute below the balloon with a similar length of cord. The parachute will stay closed until the balloon expands and bursts in the upper atmosphere. Your spaceship should then slowly float back to Earth under the parachute's open canopy.

4 **Choose your launch site and plan your flight path.** Consult an online high-altitude balloon flight predictor (such as http://predict.habhub.org) to work out the right day and location to release your spacecraft. Take care to choose a day when the winds will carry your balloon in a direction you can retrieve it. This was a real priority for us: we live on the east coast of Scotland with prevailing northeasterly winds, and without careful planning our craft could have landed in the North Sea or in Norway! Ideally you'll want to choose a launch site away from busy towns, open water, woodland, power lines, and other obstacles.

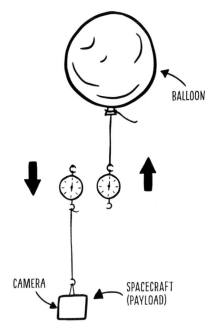

Weighing the spacecraft (payload) with a hook scale (*left*), and measuring lift with the same scale (*right*).

5 **Launch! And wait.** Make sure everything is assembled, then turn the camera and tracker on. Begin to fill the balloon with helium, using a scale to measure how much lift is being generated by the balloon. When the lift is greater than the weight of your spacecraft, stop inflating, seal the balloon, and release it. As the balloon rises into thinner air, the gas inside slowly expands until eventually, after several hours, it explodes silently in the vacuum of space. The parachute then opens, and the craft falls slowly back to Earth.

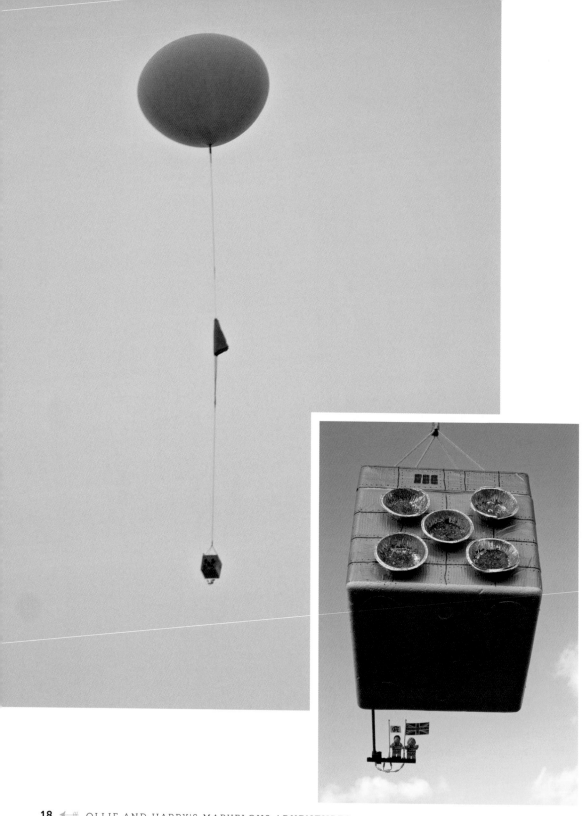

6 Recover. Your GPS tracker should pick up the craft during its descent, giving you a guide as to its landing position so that you can find it when it returns to Earth. The best part of the whole adventure is, of course, watching the images that the camera has captured. We had some amazing shots of our little Lego men hovering above Earth. You may not want to keep all three and a half hours, so perhaps use a movie-making application—and some of your favorite sci-fi film music—to edit a cool highlights film to show all your friends and family.

≫▶ **FUN FACT** A balloon can't travel into outer space because the air in Earth's atmosphere gets thinner the higher up it goes. The balloon keeps rising as long as the gas inside is lighter than the atmosphere outside. At a certain point the gas inside the balloon exceeds the pressure of the atmosphere outside, causing the balloon to burst. This normally happens at an altitude of 11 to 23 miles (18 to 37 kilometers), or 58,000 to 121,000 feet. In 2002, a balloon named BU60-1 traveled higher than any previous mission, reaching 32.9 miles (53 kilometers), or 173,900 feet.

IGLOO EXPEDITION

When a massive blizzard closed our school for a few days, we decided to explore the frozen fields around our house and build our first igloo. We loaded our equipment and food supplies onto a sled, making sure to strap everything tightly so nothing fell off. Harry learned the hard way that a packed sled will roll, and it's easy to lose your equipment! Strong waterproof boots helped us dig our feet into the snow when dragging the sled up slopes or through deep drifts. We found out very quickly that picking the route is really important as deep drifts, while great fun, will sap your strength and tire you out. We learned to read the snow to choose the ideal route.

You can build your own snowy den that will keep you snug and warm on even the coldest nights. You'll be able to cook dinner and make a hot drink with boiled snow.

What You'll Need

[ ] Warm, waterproof clothes and boots
[ ] Ski goggles or sunglasses
[ ] Hiking sticks
[ ] Sled
[ ] Rope or straps
[ ] Big, rectangular plastic container
[ ] Shovel
[ ] Ice saw or ordinary carpentry saw
[ ] Camping stove
[ ] Cooking utensils
[ ] Walrus steaks, or your food of choice

OLLIE AND HARRY'S MARVELOUS ADVENTURES

What to Do

1 **Find the best spot to build your igloo.** Choose somewhere that has a lot of hard, packed snow at least 2 feet (0.6 meter) deep. You can prod the snow with your hiking stick to test how hard it is. Try to place your igloo in a sheltered spot, as heavy winds could blow it down or cover it with snow. We picked a spot next to the woods, where the snow lay thick and we were sheltered from the wind.

WHY IGLOOS WORK

Igloos work because they are made of packed snow, not ice. As we found out, our body heat warms the air within the igloo, and it stays warm because the snow is a very good insulator. Because the snow and ice on the outside have a greater mass and higher heat capacity than the air inside, the igloo melts very, very slowly. The result is a toasty and safe structure that keeps you warm, no matter how low the temperatures get outside.

IGLOOS ARE SUPER COMFORTABLE, WE ONLY HAD ON OUR JAMMIES. AND SAUSAGE AND BEANS NEVER TASTED SO GOOD AS THEY DID INSIDE THERE.
—*Harry*

Use two hiking sticks connected by about 5 feet (1.5 m) of line to mark a circle in the snow.

2 **Mark out your igloo.** Decide how big your igloo is going to be. Do not make it any bigger than 10 feet (3 meters) across. Our first attempt was too large, and we quickly realized that smaller is better—it's difficult to make a proper dome if the base is bigger. Mark out the circle with your feet, or attach a rope roughly 5 feet (1.5 meters) long to two hiking sticks. Place one stick in the ground and outline the perimeter with the other, like a drawing compass.

3 **Make your bricks.** Using your plastic container as a mold, pack in as much snow as you can fit, pressing it down hard with the shovel. The type of snow will dictate how well this works; we found soft, sticky snow that compacted well. Turn the bricks out of the container and cut them to shape with the saw. (Make sure an adult is standing

by while you use the saw.) Your bricks should ideally be between 1 and 3 feet (0.3 to 0.9 meters) long and about 15 inches (38 centimeters) wide. Make sure they are not too heavy for you to carry and lift into position.

4 **Construct your igloo.** Lay your bricks around the marked circle. Use your saw to smooth and shape the edges so that the bricks join together nicely, then add another layer and continue upward. Each row should slope slightly inward, and you should use your saw to shape the tops of the bricks for the next layer. Make sure one person stands on the inside as you build; that person will use snow to plug any gaps from the inside. Ollie was in charge of packing the blocks and carrying them to the igloo on the sled. Harry cut the blocks and made sure that they were all leveled for the next ring of blocks.

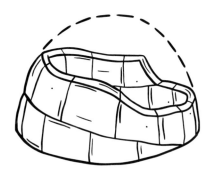

Begin by laying bricks in a circle on the ground, then add layers and continue up to form a dome.

Use a saw to shape the bricks and create a slight angle on the top of each layer, so that each row slopes in.

5 **Put on your roof cap.** Use your saw to shape the last block so it fits into the small hole at the top of the dome. Turn it on its side and push it up through the hole from the inside, then let it drop into place. Carve it into shape to fit with the rest of the ceiling. We used a couple of branches from the woods to give extra stability to the roof. Our igloo wouldn't last long during our short Scottish winter, and we didn't want heavy blocks of snow crashing down on us when we were inside.

6 **Create ventilation.** Use a hiking stick to poke a series of small air vents in the sides or at the top of your igloo to ensure clean air from outside circulates. Don't worry, it won't make your igloo cold inside. We were amazed at how warm and still our igloo was. When you are inside, your body heat causes the snow of the dome to melt and freeze again. This makes a really strong barrier between the inside and outside, so you have to make sure that carbon dioxide doesn't build up inside, as it can be dangerous.

≫→ ADVANCED ADVENTURE   You've been working really hard, so reward yourself by cooking dinner. Make sure you do this outside, as a fire would cause dangerous gas and smoke to build up inside a small igloo. Dig down to find a hard, flat surface, as the snow will melt under the stove and it could tip over. We used a small wood-burning stove, but you can use a gas camping stove or even your own small campfire. Boil some snow to make a hot drink, then cook some beans or sausages or your favorite camp food for your first ever dinner in an igloo. (We know we keep saying this, but a grown-up needs to be around when you build a fire and when you cook.)

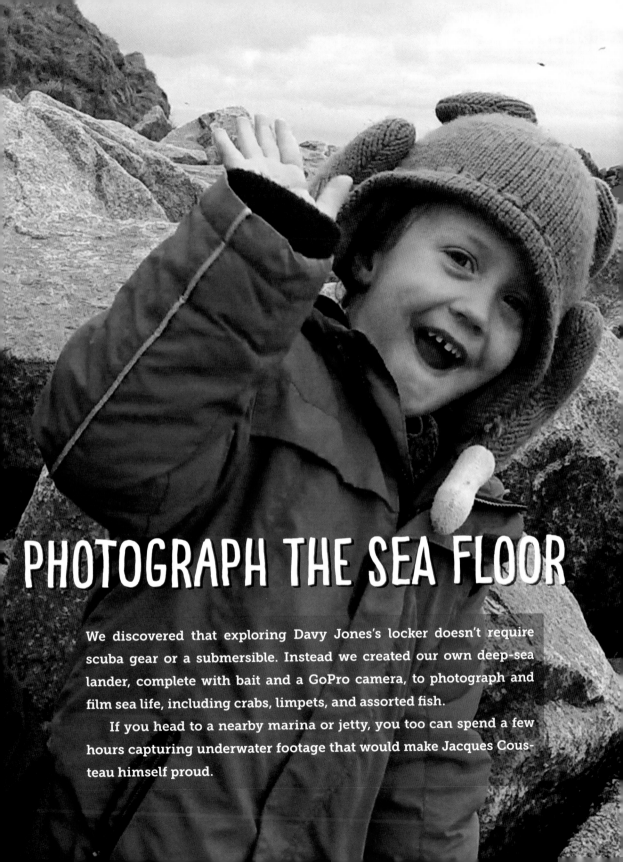

PHOTOGRAPH THE SEA FLOOR

We discovered that exploring Davy Jones's locker doesn't require scuba gear or a submersible. Instead we created our own deep-sea lander, complete with bait and a GoPro camera, to photograph and film sea life, including crabs, limpets, and assorted fish.

If you head to a nearby marina or jetty, you too can spend a few hours capturing underwater footage that would make Jacques Cousteau himself proud.

What You'll Need

[ ] GoPro or other waterproof action camera
[ ] Camera tripod
[ ] Float
[ ] Weights
[ ] Paracord (parachute cord) or similar strong line
[ ] Bait
[ ] Mesh bags
[ ] Waterproof flashlight or camera light

What to Do

1 **Assemble your lander.** Put the camera on the tripod. The tripod ensures that the camera sits up off the seabed, unobstructed by seaweed. Put weights in a mesh bag and attach it underneath so the tripod sinks feet-first into the water and attach a float at the top so it stays upright. Then attach up to 50 feet (15 meters) of line (filming any deeper will require extra lighting).

2 Prepare your bait. To attract sea life to your camera, chop up a slice or two of bacon or other bait such as chicken necks and gizzards, oily fish heads and parts, or squid pieces. Seal it in a mesh bag and tie it to the lander.

3 Dive! Set your camera to filming—you can choose to take either time-lapse images or video—and carefully lower the lander into the water, letting the line out slowly so that it eases the lander down toward the seabed. You'll know you've hit the bottom when the tension in the line loosens. Leave the camera there for 10 or 15 minutes and then carefully raise the equipment.

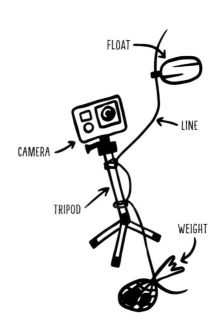

FLOAT

LINE

CAMERA

TRIPOD

WEIGHT

4 Experiment. Different environments attract different forms of sea life, so try filming in harbors, at the beach, or in deep rock pools. We don't recommend you lower the camera more than 30 feet (9 meters) into the water. You might also want to attach a waterproof flashlight for darker waters.

FUN FACT The first underwater photograph was taken in 1899 by a marine biologist and diver named Louis Boutan at a depth of 165 feet (50 meters). He had to stand still for a full 30 minutes to ensure the exposure had enough light, and he almost died from nitrogen narcosis!

DEEP-SEA DIVE

In addition to launching Lego® figures into space, we've also sent them to the bottom of the ocean. The crew and divers of a deep-sea vehicle (DSV) called *Seven Falcon* generously carried them down almost 300 feet (about 88m). We got to spend the night on the amazing high-tech vessel. We tried on dive gear, learned how to control the remotely operated vehicle (ROV), and talked to the divers in their specially sealed hypobaric chamber. We even got to have tea with the crew and spend time with the captain on the bridge.

CAPTURE RARE ANIMALS ON FILM

Living in the heart of the Scottish countryside, we are surrounded by an amazing range of wildlife, and what makes it really exciting is that so much of it remains mostly hidden from the human eye. We wanted to see if we could capture some of the more elusive creatures on film, and the results surprised us. After setting up cameras near what we thought was the home of some badgers, we caught footage of even rarer animals: pine martens.

You can experience the excitement of wildlife photography no matter where you live. Rare birds might visit your backyard, or you may be living next door to chipmunks or prairie dogs. With a little patience, research, and ingenuity, you can capture them on film.

What You'll Need

[ ] Trail camera
[ ] Binoculars or telescope
[ ] Peanut butter or other bait

What to Do

1 Find a good location. Animals, like humans, leave lots of evidence of their daily activities, so look for freshly laid paths or latrine areas. Pay attention to fresh holes or activity around the entrances to burrows, as this is a sign of an animal's presence. Animals easily pick up on scents and will be put off by any trace of your smell, so you'll need to be careful. An evening or two watching a den or burrow from a safe distance can help you choose the best location.

2 **Choose the right camera.** Trail cameras are available from hunting outfitters and online. We used a waterproof camera that works both in daylight and as an infrared camera at night. It had a motion sensor that switched the camera on and then recorded 20 seconds of video.

3 **Be discreet.** Once you've identified your spot, set up your camera. Try not to disturb the site; though it might be tempting to remain on watch, stay no longer than you need to.

PINE MARTENS HAVE A SWEET TOOTH. WE SMEARED SOME JAM AND PEANUT BUTTER INTO THE HOLES IN A ROTTEN LOG TO ENCOURAGE THESE SHY CREATURES OUT FOR A TASTY SNACK.
—*Ollie*

07:53:01 PM 2018/09/20 7 °C H68

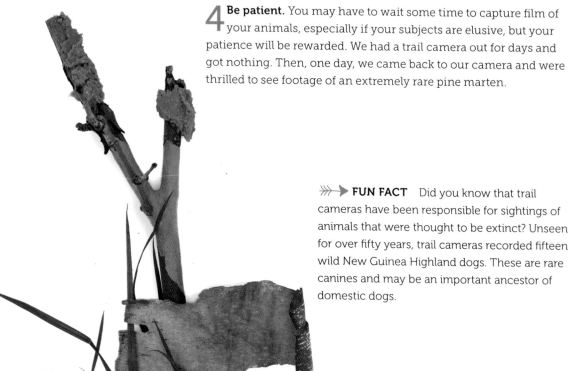

4 **Be patient.** You may have to wait some time to capture film of your animals, especially if your subjects are elusive, but your patience will be rewarded. We had a trail camera out for days and got nothing. Then, one day, we came back to our camera and were thrilled to see footage of an extremely rare pine marten.

≫→ FUN FACT Did you know that trail cameras have been responsible for sightings of animals that were thought to be extinct? Unseen for over fifty years, trail cameras recorded fifteen wild New Guinea Highland dogs. These are rare canines and may be an important ancestor of domestic dogs.

MAKE A MUMMY

Mummification sounds scary and complicated, but when we set out to preserve a dead fish, it turned out to be fun and easy. We collected our corpse from a local fishmonger and set to work, slowly and patiently drying out all moisture and wrapping it in cloth. The process took a little time, but it was nothing compared to the ten thousand years that the fish could be preserved for.

You can make your own mummy using a dead fish, some salt, and a few other ingredients. Allow yourself a few weeks to get it just right, and it will be worth the wait.

What You'll Need

[ ] Dead fish

[ ] Filleting knife

[ ] Baking powder

[ ] Table salt

[ ] Plastic container

[ ] Olive oil

[ ] Fragrant spices, such as cinnamon and nutmeg

[ ] Muslin cloth

What to Do

1 Clean the fish. Carefully cut the fish open along its underside to the gills using a sharp knife, and then scoop or scrape out the organs, leaving only muscle, skin, and bone. If you really want to copy the ancient Egyptians, you can put the organs in a "canopic jar," a glass container with a lid. We did this with the fish's heart, but we left it in salt to dry out first. If you prefer not to clean the fish yourself, a fishmonger would be happy to fillet your fish and dispose of its innards for you.

2 Make your preserving mixture. Mix two parts baking powder with one part salt in a bowl, whisking it together with a fork. Make sure to prepare enough preserving mixture, called "natron," to fill the inside of your fish at least twice.

3 Start the mummification process. Add the first layer of natron by packing it into the cavity of the fish where the organs used to be. Close the fish back up tightly afterward and cover it completely with more natron. Put the fish in a plastic container and store it in a cool place for a month. We stored ours on a bed of salt and completely covered the fish with more salt so that no air could reach it inside the container. The natron mix and salt dry out all remaining moisture in the fish so that it stops decomposing, allowing the mummification process to take place.

4 Repeat. After a month, remove the fish from the container. Open it up and carefully scrape out all the natron and dispose of it. You might want to cover your nose and mouth with a handkerchief or face mask, as it will be a little smelly! Replace the cavity of the fish with fresh natron mix, cover it in more natron, and place it back in the box and leave for another few weeks.

5 **Bury your "mummy."** Your fish should now be ready for burial. Scrape away the salt and lay the fish out on a flat surface. It should be hard and totally dried out. Brush the fish with oil before sprinkling on fragrant spices to help mask the smell (we used ground cinnamon and nutmeg). Next, cut muslin or linen cloth into strips about an inch (2.5 centmeters) wide and soak them lightly in oil. Place a folded strip or two inside the fish before closing it back up for the final time. Then carefully wrap more strips around the body so it's completely covered. The ancient Egyptians went to great lengths to bury their mummies, so we wrapped ours with gold wire to hold the muslin in place and threaded glass beads along the fish to decorate it. You can be as elaborate or as simple as you like, but make sure to store your mummy in a safe, dry place so it lasts for years to come!

> THE EGYPTIANS USED TO REGARD MUMMIFIED ANIMALS AS GOOD LUCK OMENS. HISTORIANS THINK THEY WERE PREPARED TO KEEP HUMANS COMPANY IN THE AFTERLIFE. GIANT CATACOMBS CONTAINING MILLIONS OF PREPARED ANIMALS SUCH AS CATS, COWS, AND CROCODILES HAVE BEEN DISCOVERED HIDDEN AWAY IN THE VALLEY OF THE KINGS AND OTHER SACRED BURIAL SITES IN EGYPT. "

—*Ollie*

MAGNET FISHING

We love finding lost treasure and digging up things that aren't meant to be found, so magnet fishing has us hooked. We've hauled all sorts of items out of the river near our home, from nails and horseshoes to tin cans and fishing lures. We always keep the magnet in our car so we can stop and fish if we find a potential site. Once, a friend asked us to find a pocket knife that he'd lost while fishing. The great thing about magnet fishing is that even if you turn up only a few empty cans and a broken bicycle wheel, you will have cleaned your polluted waterways!

You can go magnet fishing too. All you'll need is a long line with a superstrong magnet attached to the end. It's fun researching and discovering new locations. You never know what you'll pull out!

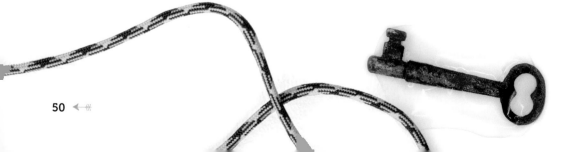

What You'll Need

[ ] Neodymium fishing magnet

[ ] Long paracord or rope

[ ] Heavy rubber gloves or work gloves

[ ] Bucket

[ ] Scraper

[ ] Wire brush

What to Do

1 Assemble your fishing magnet. Bigger magnets are stronger and work better, but don't buy a magnet that is so heavy that you won't be able to get it out of the water when it attracts objects. Attach the cord. Many fishing magnets come with a ring or eyebolt. Use a bowline or similar knot that won't come undone.

2 Select your location. Be careful about fishing in industrial areas as there might be dangerous items in the waters there. We go fishing near old bridges on the rivers and waterways near our house where lots of people cross. A harbor or marina may offer rich pickings, but someone, preferably an adult accompanying you, needs to keep an eye out for boat traffic.

Affordable, high-quality neodymium fishing magnets are available online, and magnet fishing has become a popular pastime. There are lots of YouTube videos and Facebook groups in which enthusiasts share what they have found. Most of the time, people haul out a lot of junk, like road signs and car antennas, but some magnet fishers have found rare coins, jewelry, and even antique candelabras. One Englishman caught a cash box with £100 (more than $130) inside!

4 **Explore.** Move steadily and trawl the waterway section by section. Try to avoid seaweed and plants or you'll spend more time cleaning soggy green mess off your magnet than hunting for treasure. Avoid disturbing ducks, swans, or other wildlife, especially during nesting season.

5 **Take stock.** Put aside anything valuable from your haul to research it when you get home. If you find something really old and interesting, it could end up in a museum! Whatever you do, don't put any of the metal you have recovered back into the water. Keep it in your bucket and take it to the nearest recycling center or junkyard, and you'll have helped clean up pollution.

3 **Cast your magnet.** Make sure to hold on tightly to the line. Pull it along the bottom toward you, then pull it carefully out of the water as it may have picked up rusty nails or shards of metal. Gently rest your haul on dry land and have a good look at it before touching anything. Once you've determined what's on the end of your line, put on your gloves to remove each item one at a time and place it on the ground or in your bucket. Scrape off any grass, mud, or muck with your scraper. If you've got something that looks interesting, brush it clean with the wire brush.

CATCHING LOBSTERS

We were excited when a local fisherman invited us out to catch lobsters off the coast near the town of Buchanhaven. We took turns steering the boat and together we hauled the lobster traps in and out of the water. We measured the lobsters to ensure they were big enough and helped band their big claws to avoid getting a nasty nip. We discovered that our haul of lobsters was to be sent to Balmoral Castle, where the Queen spends her time in Scotland. After an amazing day fishing, we took a lobster for dinner and cooked it on the beach over a fire.

WE'RE A CAMPING FAMILY

JUST LIKE A REGULAR FAMILY

BUT

WILDER!

OUTDOOR FEASTS AND FIRES

Cooking outdoors is one of the most fun and satisfying ways to prepare a meal. We love getting a fire going and finding different ways to cook everything from soup to sausage. Nothing tastes quite as good as a meal eaten out in the sunshine or under the stars at night, especially if you use the natural resources that surround you in your wild kitchen.

You can be an outdoor master chef too. There are lots of different cooking techniques and ways of starting fires. (But until you're way older than we are, you're going to need a grown-up with you for lighting fires and for cooking over them!)

Fire-Lighting Techniques

Bow Drill

A bow drill uses friction to generate heat and an ember. It consists of a bow, a spindle, and a notched fireboard. You place the end of the spindle in a notch in the fireboard and move the bow quickly back and forth so it spins the spindle and ignites wood dust in the notch. The ember can then be transferred to a tinder bundle made of thistle fluff and grass and blown into flames. Practice makes perfect! The best woods for a bow drill are cedar, cottonwood, willow, aspen, poplar, and buckeye. Be really careful transferring the ember: if it drops on the ground, you could start a forest fire.

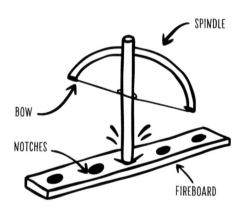

SPINDLE

BOW

NOTCHES

FIREBOARD

Magnifying Glass

In sunny weather, it's possible to start fires using the sun. Gather a small amount of dry kindling or straw and pack it into a nest. Raise a magnifying glass to it, and when you get the first hint of smoke, start blowing and fanning it to encourage flames.

Flint and Steel

For thousands of years, humans have been making fire with hard stone like flint or quartz. Using a steel striker, you can create sparks that will catch on your tinder material. This is then transferred to a grass nest or bundle and carefully blown into flames. We used amadou, created from horse hoof fungus, for our tinder material, but you can use char cloth, dry grass, or other material. Be sure to stand as far back as you can while you're doing this so that you don't singe your eyebrows!

Fire Steel

Modern fire steels are the best method for creating sparks for a fire. Matches are unreliable and can get wet, and lighters can run out of fuel after a couple of days, but a good fire steel will last for over a thousand fires. We keep one with us at all times; with dry tinder and some fatwood (resin-soaked shard of wood from the heart of a pine tree), we can start a fire almost anywhere.

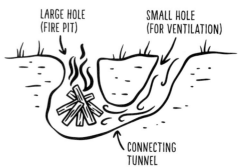

LARGE HOLE
(FIRE PIT)

SMALL HOLE
(FOR VENTILATION)

CONNECTING
TUNNEL

Dakota Fire Pit

A Dakota fire pit is an underground fire that's perfect when it's windy or you want a hidden fire. Find a spot that's flat and has soil that is easy to dig into. Clear the surrounding area of dead leaves, weeds, and other things that could spread the fire. Dig a hole to match the size of the fire you want; the bigger your hole, the bigger your fire. Dig a second, smaller hole about a foot away from the first, and use a stick or shovel to make a tunnel connecting them. (Tip: if you dig the holes at angles it will be easier to join them up. Then start your fire in the bigger hole.

Fun Outdoor Recipes and Cooking Methods

Fish on a Stick

Cooking fish is a simple pleasure, especially if you have caught them yourself. All you'll need is a solid stick that you've sharpened to a point. Clean the fish, then insert the point into the fish's mouth and through the length of its body. Use a short, Y-shaped branch to prop the skewer stick over the fire, and angle the fish next to the fire as desired. You'll know it's cooked when the skin is dark and crisp and the flesh has started to pull away from the backbone.

Spit-Roast Chicken

Skewer one or two small chickens lengthwise on a long, pointed stick. Use a couple of smaller sharpened sticks to pierce the chicken at right angles, so you can turn the spit without the chickens falling off. Next, place two Y-shaped branches in the ground a few inches (about 7 centimeters) away from each side of the fire. Place the chicken skewer so that each end of the stick is resting in the crook of the Y. Turn the chickens regularly. After an hour or so, the chickens should be cooked, but be careful to test them before eating. There should be no visible blood, and any liquids should run clear.

Hot Rock Pumpkin Soup

You can make a good cooking stove by placing rocks in a campfire, but you'll need adult supervision and careful planning. Arrange some stones (each about the size of a small orange) so that they sit deep in the embers of a roaring fire for about half an hour, or until they get really hot. Stay well away from the fire at this point: hot rocks can shatter and be dangerous. In the meantime, scoop out the inside of a pumpkin, saving the pulp. Mash the pulp in a bowl with water, a bouillon cube, and salt and pepper, then return the mix to the empty pumpkin. Test the stones' heat by flicking tiny drops of water on them—the water should sizzle if they're hot enough. Use tongs to place the rocks inside the pumpkin. They should be hot enough to bring the mixture to a boil. After it has cooled slightly, stir in 1 cup of heavy cream and enjoy.

Beach Barbecue

We love cooking on the beach. In fact, the very first adventure we ever planned we called Intergalactic Sausage Day. We still celebrate this on the first weekend of November every year, cooking sausages over a gas camping stove or, if we have time, a fire made from driftwood. The best beach dish we've ever had was a seafood feast, with freshly caught lobster that we cooked in an old cast-iron cauldron hung from a tripod. We used a metal tripod, but you can make one just as easily by planting three strong sticks solidly into the sand. We collected the lobster ourselves with a local fisherman, and with some fish, scallops, and mussels, we cooked up a feast over the white-hot coals of a small fire.

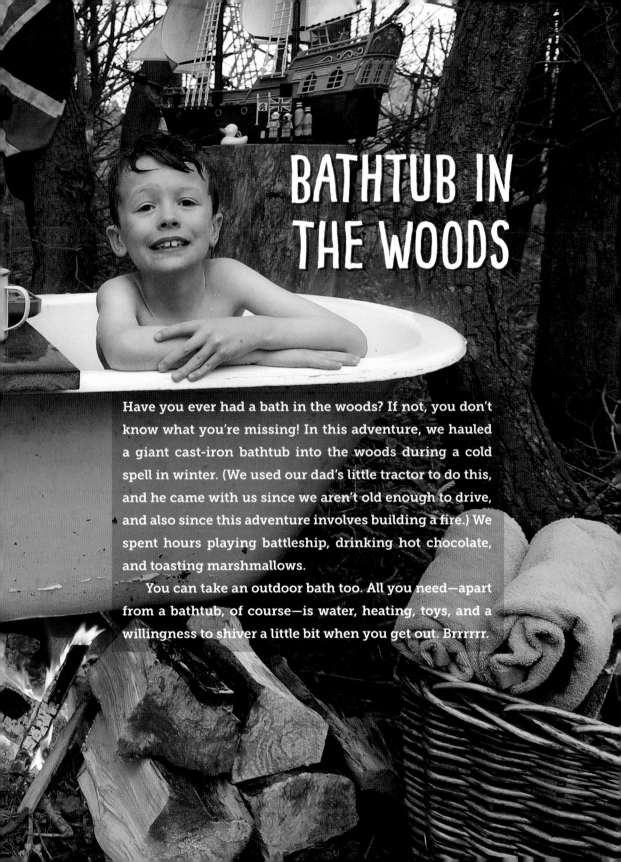

BATHTUB IN THE WOODS

Have you ever had a bath in the woods? If not, you don't know what you're missing! In this adventure, we hauled a giant cast-iron bathtub into the woods during a cold spell in winter. (We used our dad's little tractor to do this, and he came with us since we aren't old enough to drive, and also since this adventure involves building a fire.) We spent hours playing battleship, drinking hot chocolate, and toasting marshmallows.

You can take an outdoor bath too. All you need—apart from a bathtub, of course—is water, heating, toys, and a willingness to shiver a little bit when you get out. Brrrrrr.

What You'll Need

[ ] Cast-iron bathtub

[ ] Bricks, cement blocks, or logs

[ ] Wood planks

[ ] Firewood and fire-lighting material

[ ] Buckets to carry water (or a hose from a nearby faucet)

[ ] Swimming shorts and towels

[ ] Marshmallows

What to Do

1 Find a bathtub. You will need a cast-iron tub, which conducts heat. Recycling centers sometimes have old bathtubs, and you can also find them online on sites like Craigslist or eBay. (You can recycle yours afterward, if you like.)

2 Position the bathtub somewhere sheltered, where wind won't blow out your fire! Raise the bathtub on bricks, cement blocks, or logs placed under each end. You may need a couple of strong adults to give you a hand with putting them in place.

3 Build a floor for the inside of the bathtub using wooden planks. This is very important, as the bottom of the tub will get too hot to touch. Measure the length and width of the tub's floor before cutting the planks so they fit neatly, then nail or screw smaller pieces across them to fix the platform solidly in place.

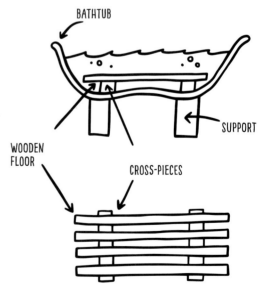

BATHTUB

SUPPORT

WOODEN FLOOR

CROSS-PIECES

4 **Start a fire beneath the bathtub.**
Be sure that the flames are directed at the underside of the tub and don't lick the sides.

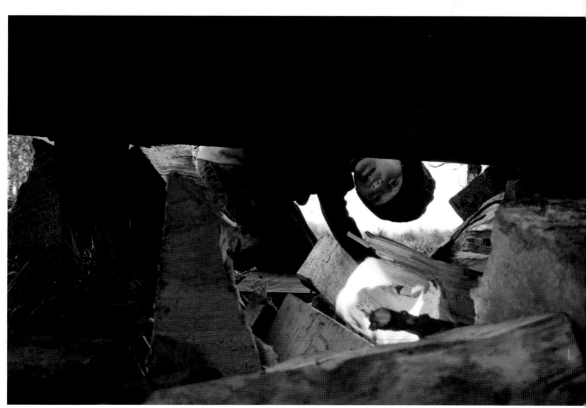

5 **Once the fire is under way, fill the bathtub with water.** We used buckets—it took ages to haul enough water from our house to the tub at the bottom of the woods in our yard. If you are near enough to a tap or faucet to be able to use a hose, this will make it a lot easier.

6 **Test the temperature of the water.** Once it's hot, you can strip down to your swimming shorts and climb in. Be careful: The outside of the tub can get really hot! If it does, douse it with water to cool it down.

7 For a tasty treat, attach some marshmallows to a long stick, carefully hold them above the fire, and roast them for a couple of minutes. Enjoy toasted marshmallows while you're having a bath!

> HAVING A WARM BATH IN THE WOODS WHEN THERE'S SNOW ON THE GROUND IS THE BEST FUN EVER. IT'S AMAZING WATCHING THE STEAM COMING OFF THE WARM WATER AS IT COLLIDES WITH THE ICY AIR.
> —Ollie

»»→ FUN FACT

The oldest bathtub ever discovered dates back more than 3,500 years ago, to 1700 BC. It was made from pottery and found in the Palace of Knossos on the Greek island of Crete.

MAKE A MEGAPULT

Catapults have been used for thousands of years, mainly for warfare. In the Middle Ages, people developed a variety of these machines to hurl arrows, boiling oil, and flaming missiles hundreds of feet through the air. We had already made handheld catapults, but Ollie decided that we needed to make a siege-level version that could fire fruit and balls around the yard.

Using some wood, rope, and elastic, you can construct your own catapult. You can also set up targets to fire at.

What You'll Need

[ ] Shovel

[ ] Several pieces of strong timber

[ ] TheraBand or similar strong elastic

[ ] Rope

[ ] Net or basket

[ ] Tennis balls, soccer balls, or old fruit

What to Do

1 Find your location. You'll need an open, private space, such as a field or big backyard, where there's no danger of hitting anyone.

2 Build your frame. The key to building a good catapult is having a strong and stable base. Dig two holes at least 2 or 3 feet (about 1 meter) deep and 3 to 4 feet (about 1 meter) apart. Place two large uprights in the holes and pack down the earth so they are firmly in place. We used timber scavenged from the woods, but you can also use long fence poles from a lumberyard.

3 Fit your launch mechanism. We used a 65-foot (20-meter) length of TheraBand, a superstrong elastic that is used by physical therapists and gyms to strengthen muscles. We wrapped it around the uprights in a big twisted loop and tied netting between the ends with cable ties. You can also use a shallow basket.

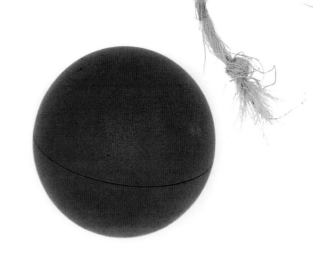

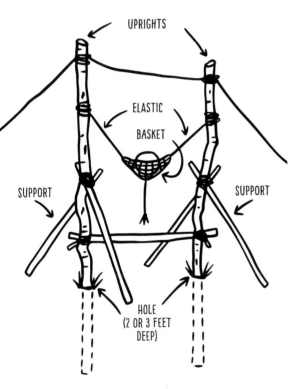

UPRIGHTS

ELASTIC

BASKET

SUPPORT

SUPPORT

HOLE
(2 OR 3 FEET
DEEP)

>>> **FUN FACT** The word "catapult" comes from the ancient Greek *kata* meaning "downward" and *pallo* meaning "to toss or hurl."

4 **Select your missiles—and targets.** You can fire all sorts of things, like tennis balls and pieces of fruit. We chose some cheap melons from the local supermarket. We spent the afternoon destroying the ramparts of our "enemy castle": a stack of plastic barrels 50 or 60 feet (15 to 18 meters) from the catapult. We had to work together to generate the pull needed to fire the melons.

> YOU CAN PLAY ALL SORTS OF GAMES WITH A GIANT CATAPULT. DOGS ALSO HAVE GREAT FUN CHASING OBJECTS FIRED FROM THE CATAPULT. UNFORTUNATELY, WE ARE BANNED FROM LAUNCHING EACH OTHER. FOR NOW, ANYWAY.
> —*Ollie & Harry*

LAST KINGS OF SCOTLAND

We love using our imaginations in our adventures, so when we were told that our ancient ancestor may have been the warrior chieftain Fergus Mor, known as the first King of Scotland, we were delighted. A friend provided us with some brilliant medieval costumes and weapons, and we used a nearby sea cave and mountain fort to stage a series of imaginary adventures, like hunting the legendary beast the Cu Sith, a giant wolf with teeth as sharp as daggers.

CROSS THE OCEAN IN A TOY BOAT

Our most famous adventure was when we put a note in a toy pirate ship, the *Adventure*, and sent it off to sea. We were amazed at what happened next.

Three months later we got an email from a couple in Denmark who had found our ship washed up in a tree after a storm. We emailed them back and they sent the boat off again, and soon it stopped in Sweden, before heading on to Norway. There, the captain of a three-masted tall ship, the *Christian Radich*, offered to take it to the coast of Africa so it could attempt to sail across the Atlantic, equipped with a tracker so that we knew its position. It had traveled 3,700 miles (6,000 kilometers) in total by the time the batteries in the GPS ran out and we lost track of it, somewhere in the Caribbean. By then, our boat had traveled halfway around the world!

You can try this, too, using a toy boat and an old-fashioned bottle, or something different. What will your message say, and where will it land?

> I LOVE THE STORY OF ROBINSON CRUSOE. IT WAS BASED ON A REAL SCOTSMAN CALLED ALEXANDER SELKIRK WHO SPENT FOUR AND A HALF YEARS MAROONED ON AN ISLAND 400 MILES OFF THE COAST OF SOUTH AMERICA.
>
> —Ollie

What You'll Need

[ ] Vessel (ship, bottle, or other watertight floating container)

[ ] Message (with email address for replies)

[ ] Rewards (Lego® figures, sweets, etc.)

[ ] Map

[ ] Notebook

[ ] Tracking device (optional)

What to Do

1 Choose your vessel. It's important to keep your message safe and dry, so we chose a toy boat with a compartment inside that we could make watertight. You can choose anything you like, such as a bottle or even a toy submarine. Whatever you pick, make sure you think about the environment. If we were to launch another ship it would be made of wood, or biodegradable plastic that will break down and dissolve into the ocean after five years. That's more than enough time for a boat to circumnavigate the world!

2 Test for seaworthiness. You need to be sure your vessel will be able to survive the high seas. Do a first trial in the bathtub at home to make sure it floats and there are no leaks that will sink it. Push the vessel under water, looking for telltale bubbles. We filled our boat with Styrofoam and filled spaces with expanding foam. We also drilled holes along the sides of the deck so that water was able to drain. (Remember what we said about having an adult with you while you drill.) Check whether your vessel will right itself if it capsizes. We added a counterweight to

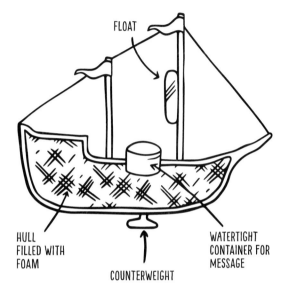

FLOAT

HULL FILLED WITH FOAM

COUNTERWEIGHT

WATERTIGHT CONTAINER FOR MESSAGE

The *Adventure*

the keel and a float to the mast to ensure that the boat turned back upright whenever it was knocked over by a wave. Repeat these tests in deeper water and see if your boat stays upright and travels in a straight line. We used an outdoor swimming pool, but you can use a small pond or stream.

3 **Write your message.** If you want people to let you know about your vessel's progress, you need to tell them who you are, where you are, and how to contact you (ask a parent if it is okay to give out this information). You also need to let them know what to do with it. Do you want them to return it to you or to the sea? Should they dispose of it? Be clear with your directions, and make sure to laminate your message and keep it in a sealed container so it doesn't get ruined.

4 **Say thank you!** Put a reward or present in with your message. It doesn't have to be much—a small toy or some hard candy is enough, but don't put in chocolate or it will melt in the sun! We used Lego® figures and wrote "Keep Me" on each of them. Three of them now live in Sweden, Denmark, and Norway after helping us out on our adventure.

5 **Launching.** It's important that the vessel sets sail from the right location and in the right conditions, otherwise it might not get very far. Be sure to select a launching site that is on open sea and away from rocks. You'll also need to check that the winds and tide are moving in the right directions. Ideally, launch when the tide and the winds are going out to sea.

ADVANCED ADVENTURE!

You can add an inexpensive GPS tracking device to your vessel that sends back its location at particular times, which you can track online, usually with a subscription. Our vessel's tracker was powered by a battery, which ran out after five months near Barbados in the Caribbean Sea. We would use a solar-powered GPS if we did it again.

KEEP ME

KEEP ME

6 **Keep a captain's log.** If you are fortunate
enough to get reports or messages on your
vessel's journey, you can record the details
in your own captain's log. Make note on its
locations and the dates and times that your
vessel made land and set off to sea again.
We looked at nautical maps and charts and
learned not just about currents and winds but
also about the geography of the *Adventure*'s
progress across the North Sea to Scandinavia
and across the Atlantic.

HERE'S THE MESSAGE WE INCLUDED IN THE *ADVENTURE*:

"Hello. Our names are Ollie and Harry
Ferguson and we live in the northeast of
Scotland. If you find this ship, please take
a photo of where you are and send it to us
at the email address below. If she is still in
good condition, could you please put her
back in the sea so she can continue her
journey. Thank you."

SAND SLEDDING

We love the snow, but what do we do when it melts during the summer? Sand sledding, of course! The Scottish coastline near us boasts miles upon miles of shifting sand dunes, but we love Forvie Sands, where a storm caused the sand dunes to swallow a whole village a few hundred years ago. The only thing that remains is the ruins of an old church that can be visited to this day. We've spent afternoons sand sledding here, sliding down the steep dunes on our plastic winter sled and snowboards. It took us a while to get the hang of it, but even if we got thrown off our sled, we were able to tumble and roll down the dunes anyway. The best part was making mounds and ramps in the sand, which we used to get some serious air.

You can easily have a sand sledding adventure. You're sure to have something lying around that can be used for a sled, and sand dunes might be closer to you than you think. . . .

What You'll Need

[ ] Sled (plastic or wood)
[ ] Rope (for pulling sledge back up steep sand dunes)
[ ] Goggles

What to Do

1 **Choose your sled.** We used a plastic snow sled, which rode down the hard-packed sand on our local dunes well, but you can use anything from cardboard to plastic trash bags. If the sand is soft and dry, you may need to choose a sled made from wood. The more polished and sleek the sled, the smoother and faster it will travel down the dunes. Goggles can be very useful to keep the sand out of your eyes, and a rope can help you haul your sled back up the slope. You can try skis or snowboards on sand, too.

> SAND SLEDS DON'T HAVE STEERING. SO I LIKE STICKING MY FEET OUT TO HELP GET UP SPEED AND DO COOL TURNS.
> —Harry

2 Choose your dunes.

Different types of sand dunes need different styles of riding. Steep, dry slopes are best, but they can take time and energy to climb. Avoid damp, north-facing dunes that don't dry out well. Take care to avoid and not damage plants or their roots as these help stabilize the dunes. Watch out for glass or other sharp debris that may be in the sand.

>>> **FUN FACT** The biggest sand dunes in North America are at Great Sand Dunes National Park in southern Colorado. The highest is 750 feet (230 meters). The sand there is so soft that walking back to the top can take five hours.

METEORITE HUNT

Earth is constantly being bombarded by meteorites—objects (mainly rocks) that have fallen from space. People often think of them as giant boulders, like the one that wiped the dinosaurs off the face of Earth, but there are thought to be small marble-sized meteorites falling within each square mile of Earth every day. We love heading out to hunt for these bits of space debris, and though it's hard work looking for them, you may be pleasantly surprised by what you're going to find.

To carry out your own meteorite hunt, you'll need a good-quality magnet similar to the one you use for Magnet Fishing (see page 49), and a lot of patience.

What You'll Need

[ ] Strong neodymium magnet
[ ] Plastic bag
[ ] Magnifying glass or microscope
[ ] Collecting box
[ ] Streak plate, unglazed ceramic, or paper

What to Do

1 **Decide where to hunt.** The best places on earth to search for meteorites are in dry climates like deserts and tundra. For most of us, though, the best places are areas with few rock formations, such as beaches, dry river beds, and fields. Always consult with the landowner if you are going onto private property. (An adult can explain what you need to do and help you do it.) Any meteorite of significant size that you find will legally belong to them.

2 **Scan the site.** Most meteorites contain large amounts of metal and can be found using a good-quality neodymium magnet. Sweep the magnet along the ground slowly and methodically until you've collected a lot of material and can start separating it. To make the process cleaner, do your sweeps with the magnet inside a plastic bag so the debris and any meteorites can be removed more readily. Get rid of any leaves, grass, and greenery, and brush off any dust or dirt .

3 **Identify your meteorite.** We've often done our victory dance a little too soon, having mistaken rusty debris for alien rock. Meteorites that have crashed to Earth recently have a black coating or "fusion crust" on them formed by the massive heat the meteorite encountered while entering Earth's atmosphere. These meteorites look glassy and smooth. Older meteorites have a smoother, dark brown coating. A real meteorite will likely contain small flecks of metal.

4 **Conduct a streak test.** Another way to test a meteorite is to use a streak plate, or a piece of unglazed ceramic. You can find streak plates online and in rock or mineral testing kits. Terrestrial rocks will leave a streak when rubbed against the surface of a streak plate, but if there is no streak or only a thin, gray mark, then the rock might be a meteorite. If you can't find a streak plate, you can use sheets of paper to conduct your test.

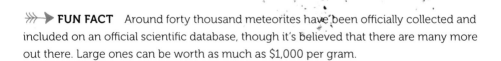

》》→ FUN FACT Around forty thousand meteorites have been officially collected and included on an official scientific database, though it's believed that there are many more out there. Large ones can be worth as much as $1,000 per gram.

MOUNTAIN HIKE

There's nothing like enjoying a meal outdoors with a spectacular view, and it's even more enjoyable at the end of a long climb. When we (with our mum and dad) hiked our local mountain, Bennachie, we collected sticks from the ancient pine forests at the foot of the mountain and gathered up some snow that was still lying in patches on the slopes. Once we reached the summit, we used our Kelly Kettle to boil the snow for a cup of hot chocolate and feasted on sandwiches and cake.

CASTING METAL TOYS

There's something special about making toys. We've cast our own spaceships, characters, animals, and vehicles using molten metal.

Put safety at the top of your list of priorities. With goggles, (make sure they fit!), safety gloves (same for these), thick jackets, and common sense (and a grown-up keeping an eye on things), there's nothing to stop you from creating your own brilliant toys.

What You'll Need

[ ] Modeling clay

[ ] Toys for molding

[ ] Ingot of pewter

[ ] Pan for melting and pouring

[ ] Knife

[ ] Safety gloves

[ ] Goggles

[ ] Cold water

[ ] Metal file

What to Do

1 **Make your molds.** Roll out the clay as you would roll out pastry dough, using a rolling pin if you'd like. Leave the clay a few inches (about 7 centimeters) thick, as it will need to hold molten metal. Next, choose the objects that you want to cast. Use objects with well-defined features, as you can lose details in the process. Press the toys into the clay so they make a perfect impression, then carefully remove them to avoid misshaping the imprint.

2 **Melt the metal.** You'll need strong heat (and a grown-up watching you!) to do this. You can use a campfire or your kitchen stove. Make sure the pan has a handle that you can hold with thick gloves. For your first attempt at casting, we suggest you use pewter because of its low melting point. Place the ingot of pewter into the pan and let it melt, gently skimming off any impurities in the molten metal with a knife.

3 Fill your molds. Put on gloves and goggles. Pick up the pan and carefully pour the molten pewter into your molds. Fill each mold almost to the top, being careful not to spill or overflow the mold. The metal will start to harden once it's removed from the heat, so work quickly. If you have any metal left over, pour it into a suitable container and let it harden to use for another day.

4 **Cool and empty your molds.** Leave your molds to stand for at least 10 minutes. Keep your gloves and goggles on to avoid potential steam scalds if the metal is still hot, and pour cold water over the molds. When the clay is cool enough to touch, flip it over and gently tap it on a hard surface so that the toys come loose from their molds. If any have stuck, gently use a knife to pry them loose. Place the toys in a bowl of water. Clean any rough edges with a metal file.

⟫▸ FUN FACT Metals such as aluminum, tin, and iron, as well as lead and copper alloys, have low melting points and are used in different forms of casting. The metal with the lowest melting point is mercury, which melts at −37.9°F (−38.8°C) and is therefore in liquid form at room temperature.

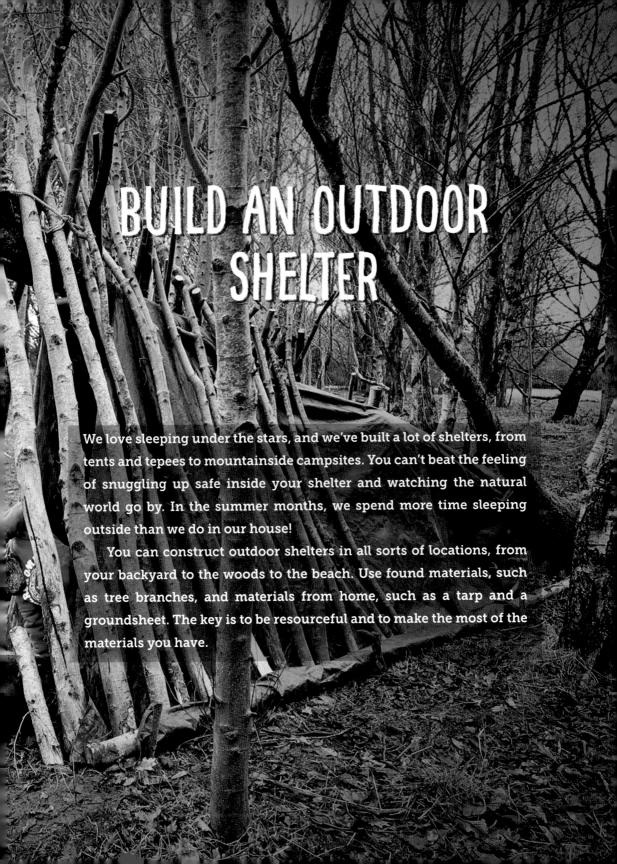

BUILD AN OUTDOOR SHELTER

We love sleeping under the stars, and we've built a lot of shelters, from tents and tepees to mountainside campsites. You can't beat the feeling of snuggling up safe inside your shelter and watching the natural world go by. In the summer months, we spend more time sleeping outside than we do in our house!

You can construct outdoor shelters in all sorts of locations, from your backyard to the woods to the beach. Use found materials, such as tree branches, and materials from home, such as a tarp and a groundsheet. The key is to be resourceful and to make the most of the materials you have.

What You'll Need

Use whatever materials are available. No matter where you set up camp, there are going to be materials at hand that you can use to construct a shelter. It might be bits of fallen timber, or discarded materials such as plastic or corrugated iron sheeting for a roof. It might be logs or old crates for tables inside your shelter. Be imaginative, but be careful not to use anyone else's property. One of our best shelters was on a beach where we used driftwood, fish boxes, and pieces of netting and other flotsam to build our camp.

What to Do

1 **Choose a location that makes the most of the landscape.** If you are building a shelter on a mountainside, use its layout to protect yourself from winds and rain. If you are in the woods, choose a hollow or utilize the canopy of the trees for protection. For our woodland shelter, we used a partially fallen tree to create a large lean-to, with sticks and poles laid on top of a waterproof tarp. On a beach, you can use rocks and dunes in the same way.

2 **Build a fire that suits the camp.** If you are in a breezy clearing or on a beach, a Dakota fire pit (see page 60) is low enough not to be affected by wind. In the woods, where you always have to be careful of fire risks, build an elevated fire and make sure it's in a clear spot away from dry leaves, grass, or twigs. Always check (or ask an adult to check) local fire risk bulletins and obey any warnings about open fires.

3 **Furnish your shelter.** We've made hammocks out of fishing nets and dining tables out of old vegetable crates. We always use a groundsheet to keep the ground dry for our sleeping bags. You can prevent heat loss and keep the bugs and critters away by making a bed frame out of wood or springy branches to keep your sleeping bag off the ground.

4 Bring your cell phone, make sure it's charged, and stay in touch with your parents or another adult. Remember that you might be out of contact for hours when you camp, so make sure to let that person know where you are and when you will be back and how they can reach you.

5 Be sure to leave the place as clean as you found it. We always take away everything we brought, and any trash left behind by others that we can carry.

OUTDOOR MOVIE NIGHT

Watching a movie is way more fun when you are outdoors. We borrowed a bedsheet and set up a cinema outside, although it didn't go down very well with Mum and Dad when we dragged the sheet through a muddy pond after. We brought out our toy cars and turned it into a drive-in, and soon the people next door were peeping over the fence, curious to see what was going on.

You can turn your backyard into a cinema with nothing more than a smartphone, a white sheet, and a homemade projector. Alternatively, you can buy an inexpensive projector that connects to a phone or computer.

What You'll Need

[ ] Magnifying glass

[ ] Shoebox

[ ] Glue or glue gun

[ ] Sheet of foam core or light plastic

[ ] Velcro or double-sided tape

[ ] Smartphone

[ ] Portable speaker (optional)

[ ] Length of cord or rope

[ ] White blanket or sheet

[ ] Clips or clothespins and bricks, rocks, or other weights

[ ] Popcorn or your choice of snack

What to Do

1 **Make your projector.** Unscrew or cut off the handle of a magnifying glass. Using the glass, trace a round hole at one short end of a shoebox. Cut it out and fit the glass into the hole. Glue around the rim of the glass so that no light seeps through. You can paint the inside of the box black, since the darker it is inside, the better the projector will work.

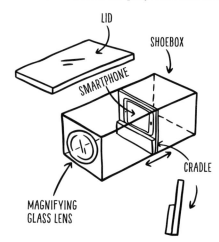

2 **Cut a piece of foam core or plastic the same size as the end of the box.** Cut one or two additional shorter pieces and glue them to the front of the first piece to cradle and support the phone. The middle of the phone screen should be at the same height as the middle of the magnifying glass lens. Attach the smartphone to the cradle using Velcro or double-sided tape. Make sure the phone is level.

3 **Set your phone's brightness to its highest level and fix the image so that it is upside down—the lens will reverse the image so that it is upright.** Focus by carefully sliding the cradle back and forth inside the box. Put the lid on the box to make sure all light leaves through the lens. If you're using a portable speaker, test the sound.

4 **Set up your theater.** Tie a line between two trees or along a fence or wall and clip your blanket or sheet to the line. It's a good idea to hang the screen somewhere sheltered so the wind doesn't blow it around, and you should anchor the bottom with a couple of bricks. We turned our cinema into a drive-in by using our favorite toy cars, but you can arrange your seating with a few lawn chairs together in a line, just like at your local movie theater. Add a few extra chairs for the neighbors!

5 **Serve your snacks and choose your movie!**

RALLY CAR DRIVING

On our most high-speed adventure, we spent a morning strapped into a stunning Ford Escort Mk1 rally championship car driven by world-class rally driver Sandy Dalgarno. He literally took us for a spin through the Scottish countryside— not that we saw much of it through our crash helmets and visors as it whizzed past at speeds of up to 60 miles per hour (100 kph). It felt twice as fast.

RAISING CHICKENS

Keeping and raising chickens can be unexpected fun, as we learned when we introduced thirty of them to our backyard in Scotland. For a start, you get to collect your own fresh, tasty eggs every day of the week. Chickens are also great for your grass and garden, gobbling up slugs and bugs from the lettuce patch. It's exciting to get to know your own brood of birds and entertaining to watch them cluck around your backyard. We started this adventure with the intention of raising them for food, but we ended up with thirty new family members. Harry even tried sneaking his beloved rooster, Ninja, into bed to cuddle at night.

You can raise and keep your own chickens. It's a job that takes a lot of responsibility, and there's a fair amount of work involved, but you'll get a lot of satisfaction from it.

Tips for Raising Chickens

Ready-made chicken houses can be purchased from feed and animal supply stores, or you can build your own (plans are widely available online), or you can adapt a garden shed or even a large wooden crate. It needs basic features including a feeder, water containers, and access to some fine grit or broken shells, which aid the chickens' digestion. Ensure your hen house has enough roosting perches and nesting boxes where hens can lay their eggs. You'll need one box for every three hens, giving your chickens as much space as possible (at least a couple square feet each). We obtained an old hen house from a local farmer, and after a good scrub and a fresh coat of paint, it was as good as new.

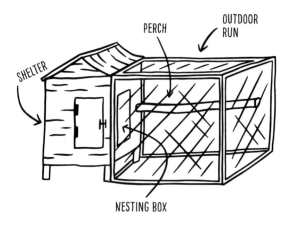

Chicken houses come in many sizes and shapes, but they all share the same basic elements.

Chickens also need to be able to move around freely and safely. We made a chicken run from the metal frame of an old plastic poly tunnel used in gardening. We covered it in chicken wire to keep it safe from foxes, a threat in our part of Scotland. We buried the chicken wire around the edges deep into the soil to prevent foxes from digging underneath.

There are many breeds of chicken, and each breed has different markings and feathers and produces different-colored eggs. Some are hardier than others, so pick chickens that are suitable for where you live. We started with a few Silkies—a rooster and a couple of hens—because they're easy to keep and are good layers. Keep the chickens inside the chicken house for the first couple of weeks. Once they're used to the house you can let them wander more widely into the chicken run and beyond.

Chickens need to be fed and watered daily. Chicken feed is readily available at pet stores and feed stores, and easily bought online. Make sure to have a "hen sitter" if you go away.

Hens will usually lay eggs throughout spring and summer and well into fall if they have enough daylight. You can expect to collect eggs once or twice a day during this period. Remember not to leave them for too long or you may end up with more chickens than you planned!

Clean the coop! Chickens produce a lot of droppings, which need to be cleaned regularly. Use a shovel and bucket. It's not the nicest job, but it makes good fertilizer for the garden.

Some basic rules to make sure you don't end up with any chicken diseases:

- Always wash your hands well with soap and water after handling your chickens and keep your hands away from your face.
- Don't let your chickens in the kitchen or anyplace where food is served.
- Don't let really little kids (under 5) handle or touch chicks, ducklings, or other live poultry without a grown-up around.
- Throw away eggs that look dirty or cracked. Don't rinse them with cold water.
- After you take the eggs from the coop, put them in the refrigerator.

> I HAD TWO SPECIAL CHICKENS, A BLACK ONE CALLED NINJA AND A GREY ONE CALLED CHICKEN NUGGET. NINJA WAS SO FRIENDLY HE SLEPT IN BED WITH ME ONCE.
> —*Harry*

TAPPING TREES

One of the coolest wilderness skills is learning how to tap a tree. Trees produce a liquid called sap, which comes in different forms. It can be so thin and watery that it is suitable for a drink, or it can be so rich and sweet that, once boiled down, it makes a delicious syrup. In Scotland, we await the rising sap in silver birch trees. In the cooler parts of North America, maple trees are tapped in late winter to make syrup and candy.

Tree tapping is a fairly straightforward process. All you need is the right timing, information, and equipment.

What You'll Need

[ ] Hand or power drill (do NOT use this without a grown-up standing with you)

[ ] Tap or spile (a hollow peg used to draw water or sap from a tree)

[ ] Bucket or other container

[ ] Muslin cloth

[ ] Wire or string

[ ] Saucepan for making syrup

[ ] Wooden plug

What to Do

1 **Find a forest or woods that has the kind of trees you want** and find out who owns it, so you can ask permission before you start.

2 **Find a tree to tap.** The best time of the year to tap a tree is in late winter or early spring. Trees store nutrients deep in their roots during the winter, but once spring begins, they redistribute these nutrients back up through the trunk and branches in the form of sap. The best-known tree for tapping is the maple. Its sap makes a rich, tasty syrup because maple sap has the highest sugar percentage of any tree sap. Trees such as sycamores, hickories, and birches produce a more watery sap that can be a refreshing drink. All of these saps can be boiled down into a syrup, however. Make sure you have identified your tree correctly. To ensure no damage is done, choose a healthy-looking tree, and avoid saplings or trees that are less than 8 inches (20 centimeters) in diameter.

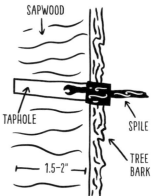

SAPWOOD

TAPHOLE

SPILE

TREE BARK

1.5–2"

3 **Check whether the tree has sap.** Stick a sharp knife into the trunk at an angle. If there is any sap, it will run down the edge of the blade.

4 Tap the tree. We made our own spile by cutting a small branch and splitting it in two. We then carved a channel down the center and tapered the end. Choose a drill bit that's the same size as your spile or tap, and drill a hole 4 feet (1.2 meters) or so above the ground, ideally on the south-facing or sunny side of the tree. Our dad helped us use a traditional carpentry drill that requires steady hand cranking. Drill the hole 1.5 to 2 inches (4 to 5 centimeters) deep. Angle the tap slightly downward, insert it into the hole, and pound it firmly into place. Use wire or string to hang a bucket on the end of the tap. The sap may flow immediately if it's a warm day, so have your bucket ready to catch it.

5 Check and empty your bucket every day. Sieve out any bits of wood or debris that might have gathered there by running the sap through a piece of muslin cloth.

6 Cook your sap. Cook your sap within a few days of gathering it so it doesn't go sour. Bring it gently to a boil, stirring it regularly. (A grown-up should be keeping an eye on you while you do this.) The sap will reduce dramatically; the syrup will be about one-fiftieth the amount of sap that you started with! As it cooks down, it will darken and sweeten. Be careful not to overcook it. Store it in clean jars.

7 Remove your taps. It's important to make sure the tree can recover from tapping, so be sure to remove the tap after a day or two. Cut a plug from a small branch the same diameter as the hole, taper the end with your knife, and tap it into the hole to seal the wound, or use a piece of a wooden dowel. You can cut the plug flush against the bark and leave no trace of damage to the tree. Carefully clean your equipment and store it away for next year's tapping season.

SAIL A KITE BOAT

On one of our wackiest adventures, we sailed a boat across a lake using a kite to pull us. We had to be patient for this one, as the weather and dark, wintery days conspired against us. It took over a week of waiting before we finally got the wind in the right direction.

You can create your own kite boat adventure with access to a boat, a safe stretch of water, and a good-quality kite.

What You'll Need

[ ] Boat, kayak, or canoe

[ ] Cody kite, or other good-quality box kite

[ ] Rope or cord

[ ] Enough wind

What to Do

1 **Put together your "kite boat."** We borrowed a stable, flat-bottomed fishing boat and built a Cody kite from a kit, but you can make your own. Take care not to make it too big, as the bigger the kite, the more pull it will have.

2 **Choose your location and time.** You'll need a safe stretch of water that you can easily navigate (and of course you need to know how to swim or you need to wear a life jacket). We used a long, thin lake owned by a trout fishery. Do NOT do this on the open sea in case the winds shift in the wrong direction and carry you offshore. Then check the weather and wait for the wind to blow in the right direction. We had to wait quite a long while, but it was worth it.

>>▶ **FUN FACT**   The first—and possibly the only—person to sail a kite boat across the English Channel was the famous inventor and aviator, Samuel Franklin Cody, in 1903. He was also the inventor of the Cody box kite, still regarded as one of the best and most efficient kites.

3 Launch. One of us sat at the front of the boat with the box kite while the other steered. We tried a few different methods for launching the kite, too. Whether it's from the boat or the shoreline, choose one that fits with your conditions and wind.

" I REALLY ENJOYED THIS ADVENTURE, PARTLY BECAUSE I COULD SPEND LOTS OF TIME FISHING WHILE WE WAITED—AND WAITED, AND WAITED—FOR THE WIND. "
—*Harry*

SAILBOAT RACING

We had one of our most educational adventures when we learned the basics of sailing during a regatta on the Moray Firth, on the northeast Scottish coast. Under the expert eyes of the commodore of the local Banff yacht club, we were shown how to tie knots, fix the rigging on a yacht, haul up different sails, steer, and tell the difference between port and starboard, fore and aft. Despite coming in second place, it was one of our happiest adventures.

HIGH-TECH TREASURE HUNT

Treasure hunting is great fun, and the modern version, geocaching, uses a GPS receiver or phone to seek out containers that have been hidden at various locations. Normally they are small waterproof containers with a logbook inside so you can record your visit. Often, people put toys or trinkets inside, and you replace whatever you take with something else. We once found twenty secret stashes in a single day—one contained a tracker that had come all the way to Scotland from Romania!

You can have a great time geocaching. We bet if you look, you will find a cache very close by. Who knows what hidden treasures you'll unearth?

What You'll Need

[ ] Cell phone or GPS tracking device

[ ] Pen or pencil

[ ] Toys or trinkets to trade

[ ] Plastic container

[ ] Small notebook

What to Do

1 **Sign up on a geocaching website.**
(Actually, at least if you live in the U.S., your parents or another adult may have to do it for you.) There's a huge, worldwide geocaching community that oversees the geocaches and their precise locations and records their activity. You will need to register with an app that helps you find caches, such as geocaching.com or opencaching.com. These are often free, but some have monthly subscriptions for more dedicated geocachers.

2 **Locate your cache.** Once you've downloaded a geocaching app, you can locate the cache nearest to you. Follow the map on your phone until you reach the right location, and then you might have to do some searching—caches are often hidden under stones or in hard-to-find spots.

3 Record your visit. Let people know you've been there by writing your name and the date and time of your discovery in the logbook. If you find something you'd like to trade in the cache, remove it and replace it with your own gift. Be generous, and try to replace like with like, but don't put anything too expensive or sentimental into the cache.

4 **Create your own cache.** The apps for the main geocaching websites will be able to guide you in setting up your own cache. Be creative! Hide it where those who find it will have had an interesting journey.

BUILD A WILDLIFE RESERVE

We love going to the zoo, but you can also build your own wildlife reservation, home to bugs, birds, squirrels, and other critters. In Scotland, we have lots of wildlife outside, so it's easy to attract creatures to our yard. We spent twenty days building a bird blind, planting wildflowers for bees, reintroducing native trees, building bat roost boxes, and creating a squirrel feeding station to help endangered red squirrels. We became the youngest people to ever receive the prestigious John Muir Conserver Award.

Here's a guide to just some of the things that you can easily build that will go a long way to attracting animals into your backyard.

Bird Feeding Station

Birds are the easiest animals to attract—the prospect of free food will draw them in without fail. You can hang bird feeders from trees in your yard or you can build a bird feeding station that will be buzzing with activity all year, especially during winter, when food is scarce.

What You'll Need

[ ] Wood

[ ] Wire mesh

[ ] String

[ ] Birdseed, nuts, fruit, etc.

What to Do

1 **Build a frame.** Place two upright pieces of wood, preferably with V shapes, in the ground. Place another piece of solid wood across the top to create a frame like soccer goal posts.

2 Hang bird feeders. You can buy bird
feeders online or at your local pet store, or
you can make them from pieces of wire mesh.
Roll the mesh into a cylinder and cut pieces
of cork or wood to fit at either end. Drill a hole
and attach a string at the top. (As we've said
before, make sure a grown-up is there when
you use a drill.) Birds love to peck at a range of
food, from nuts and seeds to special bird feed
available at pet stores and gardening centers,
so fill your bird feeder with a variety of food.
Then hang your feeder from your wooden
frame. You can also hang apples and shelled
peanuts from strings. In the winter months,
we melt suet (animal fat) in a pan and add
dried fruits, seeds, and nuts to make a thick
mixture. When it cools down, it solidifies into
a solid block of nutritious, high-energy food
for many species of birds. Be sure to hang
the feeders high so that cats, foxes, squirrels,
and other predators can't get to them. Don't
forget to put out a shallow tray of water for the
birds to drink. A ping-pong ball floating on the
surface will help prevent ice from forming in
the colder months.

**3 Observe and photograph the birds that
appear at your feeders,** then look them up
online or in a field guide to identify them. In
the spring or fall, you might even spot a rare
migrating bird on its way north or south.

Moth Trap

Moths are fascinating and beautiful creatures to observe. They're attracted to light, so it's easy to build a moth trap that will act as a magnet for these nocturnal insects.

What You'll Need

[ ] Egg cartons

[ ] Large box

[ ] Cardboard

[ ] Outdoor camping lamp or porch light

What to Do

1 **Build the trap.** Place a few egg cartons inside the box. These will provide shelter for the moths if they are trapped for a while. Using a flat piece of cardboard, make an angled trapdoor that allows the moths to fall down into the trap but prevents them from climbing out.

2 **Turn on the light.** We hung ours from a tripod and set it up in the middle of the yard. Wait until dark, then switch the light on. We left ours on overnight and checked the trap in the morning.

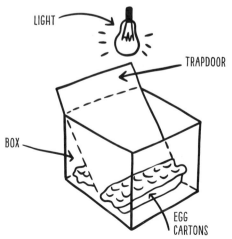

LIGHT

TRAPDOOR

BOX

EGG CARTONS

3 You can photograph the moths you collect and look them up to identify them. We saw several beautiful species, including one of our favorites, the Garden Tiger.

4 Release the moths. Carefully remove the egg cartons from the trap and scatter the moths in long grass, bushes, or other vegetation—away from hungry birds!

FLYING HAWKS

When the opportunity arose to join a professional falconer on a hunt with his two Harris's hawks, we couldn't refuse. We learned how he keeps his hawks in tip-top flying condition and the challenges he faces when hunting with them in the wild. We helped put hoods on the birds and then set off into the woods, where the hawks hunted for wild quarry. The best part of all was learning how to call the birds back to us, then watching them swoop in and land on our falconry gloves like jets on an aircraft carrier.

GIANT PAPER PLANE

We've all made paper airplanes by folding pieces of paper, but we decided to take things a step beyond that by building a giant craft capable of flying much farther than a few feet. We launched our giant paper plane from high on a hill next to the remains of an ancient fort called Dunnideer Castle. It took three of us to launch it, but with the help of our Mum and some gusts of wind, our plane took to the skies like a Highland eagle.

You can pilot your own giant paper plane and watch it soar into the air before landing back on Earth.

What You'll Need

[ ] Cardboard
[ ] Scissors or craft knife
[ ] Strong duct tape

What to Do

1 **Choose the best material.** At first, we tried to make our plane from the biggest sheet of paper we could find. At 10 by 16 feet (3 by 5 meters), we thought we had found the perfect piece, but the plane we constructed in our school gymnasium collapsed under its own weight before it could get off the ground. Eventually we opted for a 10-foot (3-meter) cardboard plane design instead, using cardboard from strong, rigid packing boxes.

≫▶ FUN FACTS   The largest paper plane ever made was 45 feet (13.7 meters) long with a wingspan of 24 feet (7.3 meters). It weighed 800 pounds (363 kilograms) and was named *Arturo's Desert Eagle* after its designer, a 12-year-old from Arizona named Arturo Valdenegro.

The longest paper plane flight is 226 feet 10 inches (69.14 meters), set in 2012. The plane was designed by John Collins, known as "The Paper Plane Guy" and thrown by former football player Joe Ayoob at McClellan Air Force Base in California.

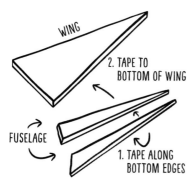

The plane is made from three large triangular pieces, joined with duct tape.

2 **Cut out the shape.** You'll need to make three triangles—one large triangle for the wing and two narrower triangles for the fuselage. Tape the two narrower pieces together along their length, then position them under the wing triangle in a V shape to increase rigidity in the fuselage and make it strong during launch. Tape it into place with duct tape. Seal the sections together and make sure there are no gaps that could affect the plane's aerodynamics.

3 **Choose a launch pad.** Launch your plane from the highest point you can find. To prepare for launch, use a flag or piece of cloth to figure out which way the wind is blowing. You want to launch your plane so it glides into a very gentle wind to give the plane lift, but be careful of strong updrafts. A strong updraft may push the plane back into the hill or behind you. The wind blowing from behind you will work well, as it will take the plane a long way down the hill.

4 **Launch your plane.** It might take two or three people to hold it, one at each end of the fuselage below the wings. Try to launch the plane slightly upward. If your first flight doesn't succeed, try again—you'll soon learn what's required to make your plane really fly. Try cutting flaps in the wings to increase lift if it seems nose-heavy.

Acknowledgments

Writing this book has been an adventure in itself. In fact, it's been as unlikely and surprising as any of the challenges we've taken on these past few years. So we can't let this opportunity pass without thanking those who have made it possible.

It all began in 2016 when we were approached unexpectedly by the writer Garry Jenkins. We were slightly taken by surprise when he suggested our adventures were worthy of a book, but his instincts have proven right and he has guided us through the sometimes daunting process every step of the way. He's even participated in an adventure or two himself during a visit to Scotland. The next vote of thanks must go to our agent, Lucy Cleland, at Kneerim & Williams in Boston. She too approached us out of the blue, having spotted from across the Atlantic the potential for a book that would inspire and hopefully entertain young readers not just in the US and the UK, but around the world. Since then she has been a fount of sound advice and support, helping us to craft a book and then steering us toward W. W. Norton and our publisher, Simon Boughton. We've loved working with Simon and his team in New York, in particular Kristin Allard, who helped us through the editorial process. Simon's enthusiasm for adventuring—and Scotland—has been infectious and is reflected in the beautiful book he and his team have produced.

Last—but definitely not least—we'd like to thank the many people who have helped us bring our crazy ideas to fruition. From those who have lent us equipment or expertise, to those who have simply cheered us on from the sidelines on social media or elsewhere, you've all helped us more than you can know. Some have gone to extraordinary lengths to help us. You do know who you are and—we hope—you also know how much we appreciate all that you have done.

—The Ferguson Family, Aberdeenshire, 2019